MW00882792

WOULD YOU RATHER

FOR GIRLS, BY GIRLS

300+ FUN, KID APPROVED
QUESTIONS
FOR LOTS OF LAUGHS

ALEXA SCHLESINGER

Copyright 2023 © Calm Waters Publishing House
All Rights Reserved
The contents of this book may not be reproduced, duplicated or
transmitted without direct written permission from the author.
Under no circumstances will any legal responsibility or blame be
held against the publisher for any reparation, damages,
or monetary loss due to the information herein,
either directly or indirectly.

Legal Notice:
This book is copyright protected. This is only for personal use.
You cannot amend, distribute, sell, use, quote or
paraphrase any part or
the content within this book without the consent of the author.

Disclaimer Notice:
Please note the information contained within this document is
for educational and entertainment purposes only. Every attempt
has been made to provide accurate,
up to date and reliable complete information.
No warranties of any kind are expressed or implied. Readers
acknowledge that the author is not engaging in the rendering
of legal, financial, medical or professional advice.
The content of this book has been derived from
various sources. Please consult a licensed professional before
attempting any techniques outlined in this book.
By reading this document, the reader agrees that under no
circumstances is the author responsible for any losses,
direct or indirect, which are incurred as a result of the use of
information contained within this document, including, but not
limited to, —errors, omissions, or inaccuracies.

Format and layout design by Sunil Nissanka A.

CONTENTS

CONTENTS

INTRODUCTION

Would you rather miss out on a book filled with super fun questions or dive into it from cover to cover? If you chose to explore every page, you've got it right in your hands!

This book is your go-to for all things fun, from fashion and food to friends and a sprinkle of silliness and a dash of ickiness – because, after all, it's "Would You Rather"!

Whether it's a sleepover, a road trip, or just hanging out with friends, this book will turn good times into great times. Read it all at once, or savor it one question at a time. Think you know everything about your friends? Try predicting their answers.

Pass it around and take turns asking questions, or you can be the ultimate Question Queen! No matter how you use it, one thing is for sure – these questions will spark hours of giggles, a few gross-outs, and maybe even some deep thoughts. Get ready for a world of laughs and surprises!

SHOUT-OUTS

Big thanks to my awesome mom, who helped me with those touches only the best mom could add. She kept me hyped through the whole process. I couldn't have done it without her constant good vibes and support!

And huge thanks to my cousin, Jada Jacobelli, for dropping some clever, creative, and interesting questions that gave the book that extra boost. Jada, you're the MVP for bringing your cool ideas to the book and making this project much more fun and exciting.

Mom, Jada, you two are the best! Much love!

MORTIFYING MOMENTS

Ready to cringe? Get set for some hilariously embarrassing moments! Don't fret; it's all in good fun. When life gets a little awkward, just remember, it could always be worse, right?

WOULD YOU RATHER?

Would you rather be caught off mute during an online class while singing loudly **OR** be caught asleep and snoring for everyone to hear?

Would you rather fart loudly enough that everyone around you laughs **OR** be the only one laughing like crazy when someone else farts?

Would you rather sing instead of speak **OR** wear your socks on your hands for one whole day at school?

WOULD YOU RATHER?

Would you rather throw up in front of your favorite celebrity **OR** forget the words of a song you're performing on live television?

Would you rather have your parents sing in front of your school **OR** follow you for an entire school day trying to act cool?

Would you rather have to eat an entire meal as everyone in your class just watches **OR** beatbox in front of your class?

WOULD YOU RATHER?

Would you rather bark like a dog every time your teacher calls your name in school **OR** make a fish face whenever your teacher asks a question?

Would you rather wear your underwear over your pants for one day **OR** wear a tuxedo for a day?

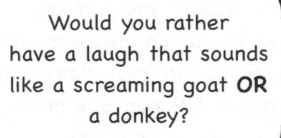

Would you rather have a laugh that sounds like a screaming goat **OR** a donkey?

WOULD YOU RATHER?

Would you rather switch clothes with your dad **OR** wear "grandma clothes"?

Would you rather say the wrong answer every time the teacher asks you a question **OR** get everyone's name wrong at school?

Would you rather sneeze snot all over the place **OR** laugh so hard you pee a little?

WOULD YOU RATHER?

Would you rather
call your teacher "mom" **OR**
hug a stranger you thought
was your friend?

Would you rather
break into song in the middle
of class **OR** only wear formal
dresses for the rest of the
school year?

Would you rather
have every second of your life
broadcasted online **OR** never
watch an online
video again?

WOULD YOU RATHER?

Would you rather admit to your brother's friend that you think he's cute **OR** start dancing randomly by yourself in front of him?

Would you rather not be able to talk for a year **OR** give up the ability to taste food for a year?

Would you rather have to include your squishy toy pet in every photo you ever take **OR** never get to cuddle with it again?

WOULD YOU RATHER?

Would you rather sing every word you say **OR** talk in a very high-pitched voice?

Would you rather walk around with broccoli stuck in your teeth **OR** toilet paper coming out of your pants?

Would you rather have your mom perform a rap in choir class **OR** your dad perform an interpretive dance in gym class?

WOULD YOU RATHER?

Would you rather never wash your hair again **OR** never brush your teeth again?

Would you rather talk in your sleep **OR** fall asleep in the middle of conversations?

Would you rather spill chocolate milk down the front of your sweater **OR** accidentally sit in a puddle of soup?

WOULD YOU RATHER?

Would you rather have a silly school picture every year **OR** have to dance in every school talent show?

Would you rather wear a sign that says, 'kick me' **OR** 'hug me'?

Would you rather have silent but horrible smelling farts **OR** really loud farts that smell like flowers?

FRIENDS, FAMILY
&
CRUSHES

They're all your favorites and
the ones you adore, but let's be
real – they can drive you a bit
nutty sometimes, right?
No worries. We've got questions
that dive into all the fun stuff
too!

WOULD YOU RATHER?

Would you rather have a sleepover with one of your best friends **OR** invite eight other girls over you'd like to get to know better?

Would you rather prank your parents **OR** toilet paper your neighbor's house during your next sleepover?

Would you rather have to clean your home for all of your family every day **OR** cook for your family every day?

XO!

WOULD YOU RATHER?

Would you rather
be an only child **OR** have
a ton of brothers and
sisters?

Would you rather
have 10 younger siblings **OR**
10 older siblings?

Would you rather
have all sisters **OR** all
brothers?

WOULD YOU RATHER?

Would you rather go on a family vacation to your favorite amusement park **OR** to a city you've always wanted to see?

Would you rather be best friends with your favorite musician **OR** with your favorite movie star?

Would you rather have to tell your parents all of your secrets **OR** let your classmates read them out of a book?

WOULD YOU RATHER?

Would you rather have your parents **OR** your friends tell your crush that you like them?

Would you rather be a bully **OR** stand up for someone who is getting bullied?

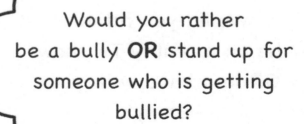

Would you rather someone tell you that you're just like your mom **OR** your dad?

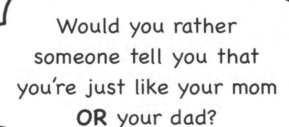

WOULD YOU RATHER?

Would you rather copy all of your friend's clothes for one week without telling them **OR** ignore your friend for a week with no explanation?

Would you rather be on a reality TV show **OR** in a band with your family?

Would you rather have a famous parent **OR** be a child star?

WOULD YOU RATHER?

Would you rather switch family homes with your best friend for a week **OR** switch parents?

Would you rather go back in time and meet your grandparents as kids **OR** go into the future and meet your grandkids as adults?

Would you rather be friends with someone who is extremely funny but a little mean **OR** extremely kind but not funny?

WOULD YOU RATHER?

Would you rather go on a road trip with your family **OR** with your friends?

Would you rather your crush **OR** your mom read your diary?

Would you rather take an awkward family photo wearing matching pajamas **OR** matching sweaters?

WOULD YOU RATHER?

Would you rather cheer your best friend on at a sporting event **OR** have your best friend cheer you on at a sporting event?

Would you rather get advice from your mom **OR** your best friend?

Would you rather be a mean girl **OR** stand up to one?

WOULD YOU RATHER?

Would you rather babysit your best friend's little sister for free **OR** your worst enemy's little sister for $50 an hour?

Would you rather go to a dance with your friends **OR** with your crush?

Would you rather give a friendship bracelet to your worst enemy **OR** a random stranger on the street?

WOULD YOU RATHER?

Would you rather stand up for your opinion in a friend group if it's different than everyone else's **OR** pretend to have the same opinion as them?

Would you rather have a friend who brings you on cool vacations but is rude to you **OR** a friend who does normal stuff but always has your back?

Would you rather be able to read your dog's mind **OR** your best friend's mind?

23

WOULD YOU RATHER?

Would you rather have a group of aunts who are always very loud and rambunctious **OR** who are very serious and quiet?

Would you rather share a big room with a mini-refrigerator and wifi with your sibling **OR** have your own room without any of those extras?

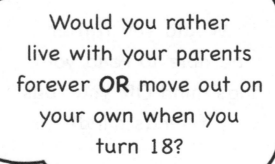

Would you rather live with your parents forever **OR** move out on your own when you turn 18?

SPORTS, GAMES
&
HOBBIES

Lace up your sneakers, pick up that controller, or grab your art supplies because it's game time! What's your favorite way to have fun? Whether it is crafting, cooking, sports, or music, we've got questions to get your mind racing!

WOULD YOU RATHER?

Would you rather get paid to play your favorite sport **OR** your favorite video game?

Would you rather play pro tennis **OR** pro golf?

Would you rather beat the world's best chess player **OR** the world's best poker player?

WOULD YOU RATHER?

Would you rather
have perfect aim **OR**
super speed?

Would you rather
be a famous ice skater **OR**
a famous archer?

Would you rather
play a soccer game where the
ball is on fire **OR** play hockey
while riding a unicycle?

WOULD YOU RATHER?

Would you rather
do synchronized
swimming **OR** ballet?

Would you rather
be able to draw exactly what
you see **OR** invent a new
style of painting?

Would you rather
be the best dodgeball player
on a mediocre team **OR** a
mediocre dodgeball player on
an amazing team?

WOULD YOU RATHER?

Would you rather perform with the cheerleaders **OR** join the football players on the field?

Would you rather crochet an animal **OR** knit a scarf?

Would you rather wake up knowing how to speak a new language **OR** with the ability to read twice as fast as you can now?

WOULD YOU RATHER?

Would you rather have the lead in the school play **OR** be the star of the basketball team?

Would you rather be able to sew an entire outfit **OR** bake your own cupcakes?

Would you rather spend $500 on friendship bracelet supplies **OR** $500 on makeup?

WOULD YOU RATHER?

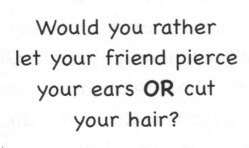

Would you rather
let your friend pierce
your ears **OR** cut
your hair?

Would you rather
miss the winning shot in
a basketball game **OR**
forget your lines
in a play?

Would you rather
be able to do a back
handspring **OR**
an aerial?

WOULD YOU RATHER?

Would you rather be at the top of the cheerleading pyramid **OR** be the cheerleader who gets thrown in the air during stunts?

Would you rather be able to paint beautiful pictures **OR** make beautiful music?

Would you rather laugh at other people's jokes **OR** have other people laugh at your jokes?

PETS
&
ANIMALS

Aww, major cute alert! We're not talking about your celebrity crush here – we're all about our furry (and maybe a few fishy) pals! These questions might be a paw-some challenge, but you've got to have a favorite, right?

WOULD YOU RATHER?

Would you rather show up to your school dance riding an ostrich **OR** a donkey?

Would you rather have a tamed tiger **OR** a tamed Komodo dragon as a pet?

Would you rather have the ability to talk to dogs **OR** to fly with birds?

WOULD YOU RATHER?

Would you rather be able to safely hug a monkey **OR** a panda bear?

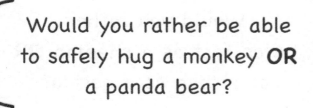

Would you rather have a cat tail **OR** dog ears?

Would you rather have a horse that could talk **OR** a horse that could fly?

35

WOULD YOU RATHER?

Would you rather
be as fast as a cheetah **OR**
as strong as a gorilla?

Would you rather
ride in a race on a horse
OR a dolphin?

Would you rather
be a dog **OR** a cat for
one week?

WOULD YOU RATHER?

Would you rather spend a night at an aquarium **OR** in a butterfly conservatory?

Would you rather shear a sheep **OR** milk a goat?

Would you rather have access to fresh eggs from your own chicken **OR** fresh milk from your own cow?

WOULD YOU RATHER?

Would you rather be able to ride in a kangaroo pouch **OR** be carried around by a large bird?

Would you rather have a cat's retractable claws **OR** an owl's ability to see at night?

Would you rather spend a day at the zoo **OR** go on a safari?

WOULD YOU RATHER?

Would you rather adopt a rambunctious puppy **OR** a quiet, older dog?

Would you rather have a pet capybara **OR** a pet sloth?

Would you rather snuggle with a porcupine **OR** with a skunk?

WOULD YOU RATHER?

Would you rather have 50 dogs **OR** 25 cats living in your house?

Would you rather have a rare hot pink fish **OR** a rare electric blue lizard?

Would you rather star in a show where you handled snakes **OR** cuddled tarantulas?

WOULD YOU RATHER?

Would you rather fly on the wings of an eagle **OR** swim on a whale's back?

Would you rather have a dog that stays a puppy forever **OR** a cat that stays a kitten forever?

Would you rather have a baby goat farm **OR** a baby bunny farm?

WOULD YOU RATHER?

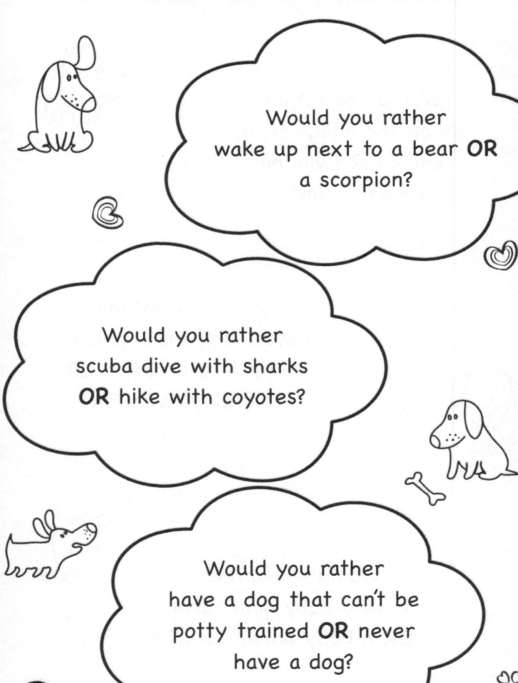

Would you rather wake up next to a bear **OR** a scorpion?

Would you rather scuba dive with sharks **OR** hike with coyotes?

Would you rather have a dog that can't be potty trained **OR** never have a dog?

FOOD

Salty or sweet? Hot or cold?
Yuck or yum? It's your call!
These questions will help you
discover your taste preferences
and what turns your stomach.
And you might even find a few
tasty surprises!

WOULD YOU RATHER?

Would you rather
be a famous chef **OR**
a famous baker?

Would you rather
drink milk with hot sauce and
mayonnaise **OR** pickle juice with
maple syrup and lard at
dinner every day?

Would you rather
taste the world's best ice
cream **OR** the world's best
cookie?

WOULD YOU RATHER?

Would you rather live in a world without french fries **OR** pizza?

Would you rather always get pineapples **OR** anchovies on your pizza?

Would you rather never have condiments again **OR** have to put condiments on everything you eat?

WOULD YOU RATHER?

Would you rather
have a personal chef **OR**
be an excellent cook?

Would you rather
be allergic to cheese **OR**
bread?

Would you rather
give up dessert **OR**
all fried foods?

WOULD YOU RATHER?

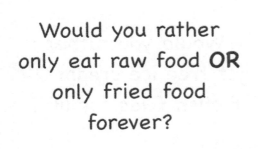

Would you rather
only eat raw food **OR**
only fried food
forever?

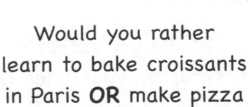

Would you rather
learn to bake croissants
in Paris **OR** make pizza
in Naples?

Would you rather
never eat ice cream again
OR eat only ice cream for
a whole year?

WOULD YOU RATHER?

Would you rather
get free ice cream **OR**
french fries for life?

Would you rather
put syrup on your fries **OR**
ketchup on your waffles?

Would you rather
cut out sweets **OR** salty
snacks forever?

WOULD YOU RATHER?

Would you rather
have a water bottle the size
of a gallon jug **OR**
a baby bottle?

Would you rather
drink hot soda **OR**
eat cold soup?

Would you rather
only be able to eat
with your hands **OR**
with chopsticks?

WOULD YOU RATHER?

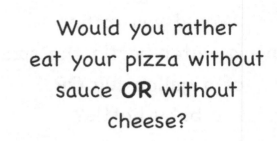

Would you rather
eat your pizza without
sauce **OR** without
cheese?

Would you rather
never get to cook again **OR**
never get to bake again?

Would you rather
have cereal for dinner **OR**
pizza for breakfast?

SHOPPING, CLOTHES
&
FASHION

Get ready for some seriously stylish dilemmas. Making fashion decisions is hard enough – who can honestly choose between your best hair days and perfectly polished nails? Good luck, because you're in for some fashionable fun!

WOULD YOU RATHER?

Would you rather style your favorite celebrity for a week **OR** have a celebrity stylist choose outfits for you?

Would you rather design your own clothes **OR** have a famous designer design custom-made clothes for you?

Would you rather buy all your clothes from stores in Paris **OR** in New York City?

WOULD YOU RATHER?

Would you rather
go to school after applying
makeup without a mirror **OR**
after picking out clothes in
complete darkness?

Would you rather
go to Fashion Week
in Paris **OR**
the Met Gala in NYC?

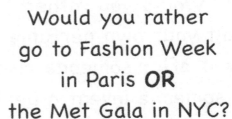

Would you rather
have $5,000 to go shopping
at a bargain store **OR**
$300 to go shopping at a
store in the mall?

WOULD YOU RATHER?

Would you rather start your own clothing brand **OR** makeup line?

Would you rather invent your own perfume and name it after someone else **OR** have someone invent a perfume that's named after you?

Would you rather dress in all black **OR** all pink for a week?

WOULD YOU RATHER?

Would you rather
have to use a bright
yellow umbrella **OR** wear
bright red rain boots
every time it rains?

Would you rather
wear a cape **OR** a bonnet
to school for a week?

Would you rather
go to school dressed like
a superhero every day
for a week **OR** wear the
same outfit three days
in a row?

WOULD YOU RATHER?

Would you rather have an endless shopping spree at the biggest beauty store **OR** get free sneakers for life?

Would you rather have your dad paint your nails **OR** braid your hair?

Would you rather get to test every new shoe from your favorite brand **OR** every new lip gloss from your favorite brand?

WOULD YOU RATHER?

Would you rather have a backpack that always has the perfect outfit for any occasion inside **OR** a closet full of clothes that change color with your emotions?

Would you rather design your own line of bags **OR** shoes?

Would you rather wear high heels in the snow **OR** in the sand?

WOULD YOU RATHER?

Would you rather wear seven earrings in each ear **OR** never wear earrings at all?

Would you rather wear an outfit from your principal's closet **OR** your grandfather's closet?

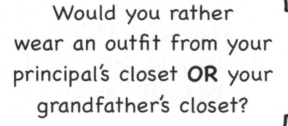

Would you rather have hair down to your ankles **OR** just past the bottom of your ears?

WOULD YOU RATHER?

Would you rather pick your best friend's outfits for a week **OR** have your best friend choose yours for a week?

Would you rather wear sweats to a formal dance **OR** a formal dress to the grocery store?

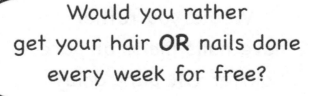

Would you rather get your hair **OR** nails done every week for free?

WOULD YOU RATHER?

Would you rather
wear a bathing suit in really
cold weather **OR**
a sweatshirt and coat in
really hot weather?

Would you rather
wear body lotion that smells
like garlic **OR** pepperoni?

Would you rather
have nails made of pure
glitter **OR** pure gold?

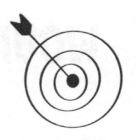

GOALS, PLANS
&
DREAMS

Dreaming about the future is
like riding a rocket to
awesomeness! Your destination?
It's amazing, and it's all in your
hands. Let these questions help
you pave the way to a
life-changing journey!

WOULD YOU RATHER?

Would you rather work at your favorite clothing store **OR** your favorite restaurant?

Would you rather be a famous cake designer **OR** a backup dancer for a musician?

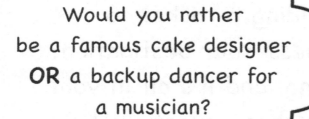

Would you rather get rich from the stock market **OR** from an embarrassing viral video?

WOULD YOU RATHER?

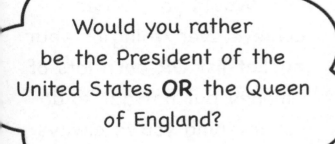

Would you rather be the President of the United States **OR** the Queen of England?

Would you rather end world hunger **OR** put a stop to all wars?

Would you rather have a job helping animals **OR** babies?

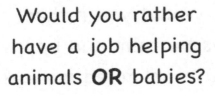

WOULD YOU RATHER?

Would you rather achieve everything on your bucket list **OR** earn lots of money but not get to do everything you've always wanted to?

Would you rather turn your favorite hobby into a career **OR** get paid to do nothing?

Would you rather always be calm and happy **OR** have unlimited money?

WOULD YOU RATHER?

Would you rather
be recognized for performing
a good service for humanity
OR be known for getting in
trouble all the time?

Would you rather
know what's going to happen
in your future **OR** forget
everything immediately
after it happens?

Would you rather
spend your time studying
to be a doctor **OR**
a business owner?

WOULD YOU RATHER?

Would you rather become the first female President of the United States **OR** the first female head coach of a professional football team?

Would you rather be a famous singer **OR** a famous movie star?

Would you rather teach yoga on a beautiful beach **OR** teach skiing in the mountains?

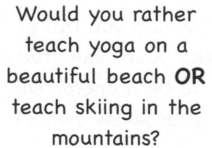

WOULD YOU RATHER?

Would you rather
have a vacation home in
the mountains **OR**
on a beach?

Would you rather
win an Olympic medal **OR**
an Oscar?

Would you rather
be able to speak Chinese **OR**
communicate with sign
language?

WOULD YOU RATHER?

Would you rather be really rich **OR** really famous?

Would you rather publish a book **OR** record an album?

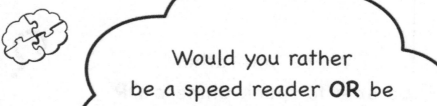

Would you rather be a speed reader **OR** be able to type really, really fast?

WOULD YOU RATHER?

Would you rather
be able to play the guitar
OR the piano?

Would you rather
have a Guinness World
Record **OR**
a Nobel Prize?

Would you rather
be given all the money
you will ever need **OR**
work for it?

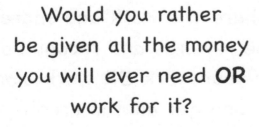

WOULD YOU RATHER?

Would you rather achieve one big goal without experiencing any failure **OR** achieve five big goals, but fail many times on your path to success?

Would you rather live without any stress and no big dreams or aspirations **OR** have major goals but feel some stress as you work toward them?

Would you rather share the work and share the rewards and recognition for your work **OR** work alone and get all the credit all the time?

TRAVEL
&
ADVENTURES

Juggling travel in your jam-packed schedule can be tough, but don't fret! We've got your adventure plans covered with these thrilling questions. Buckle up – we're off to parts unknown, and who knows where the journey will lead!

WOULD YOU RATHER?

Would you rather go to a boarding school in England **OR** travel to Italy every summer with your family?

Would you rather go skydiving **OR** ride all day in a hot air balloon?

Would you rather visit the Eiffel Tower **OR** Big Ben?

WOULD YOU RATHER?

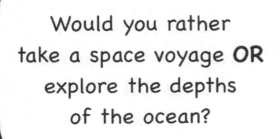

Would you rather
take a space voyage **OR**
explore the depths
of the ocean?

Would you rather
visit every country in
Europe **OR** visit every
state in the US?

Would you rather
see a live alien **OR**
a new species of
sea monster?

WOULD YOU RATHER?

Would you rather discover a new animal species **OR** a new planet?

Would you rather have a star named after you **OR** a hurricane named after you?

Would you rather travel through the desert by camel **OR** over mountains on a goat?

WOULD YOU RATHER?

Would you rather
go on an African safari **OR**
snorkel in Australia's Great
Barrier Reef?

Would you rather
explore an underwater
cavern **OR** underwater ship
wreckage?

Would you rather
visit a new continent **OR**
explore a new part of
your town?

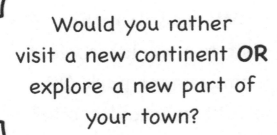

WOULD YOU RATHER?

Would you rather walk the red carpet at a movie premiere **OR** spend a weekend in your favorite national park?

Would you rather drive 12 hours in a car and be able to stop whenever you want **OR** fly two hours in a plane with a broken bathroom?

Would you rather visit the world's coolest amusement park **OR** a 300 year-old castle?

WOULD YOU RATHER?

Would you rather control something that happens in the future **OR** change one thing about the past?

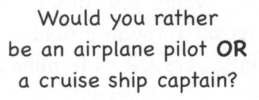

Would you rather be an airplane pilot **OR** a cruise ship captain?

Would you rather go on a fancy cruise **OR** stay at a luxury resort?

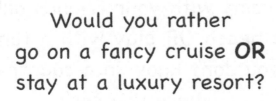

WOULD YOU RATHER?

Would you rather stay in a haunted hotel **OR** in an extremely gross hotel?

Would you rather stroll through a field of sunflowers **OR** walk beneath a rainbow?

Would you rather camp with your friends on the beach **OR** stay with a family you don't know in a country where you can't speak the language?

HOLIDAYS, BIRTHDAYS
&
CELEBRATIONS

From secret Valentines to
Christmas melodies and
Halloween thrills, these
holidays are super exciting!
But the catch is, you have to
choose! No matter what you
pick, it's guaranteed to be
a blast!

WOULD YOU RATHER?

Would you rather
have your parents buy you
a gift from your favorite store
every year **OR** have them
surprise you?

Would you rather
ask your friends for birthday
presents **OR** donations to
a charity that is special
to you?

Would you rather
give up Christmas cookies **OR**
Halloween candy forever?

WOULD YOU RATHER?

Would you rather live without holiday lights **OR** holiday music?

Would you rather skip Halloween **OR** your birthday next year?

Would you rather go Christmas caroling on Christmas Eve **OR** spend Christmas Day volunteering at a homeless shelter with your family?

WOULD YOU RATHER?

Would you rather
get money **OR** presents on
your birthday?

Would you rather
give up mashed potatoes **OR**
stuffing on Thanksgiving?

Would you rather
have a birthday cake that's
filled with mud **OR** receive no
birthday presents?

WOULD YOU RATHER?

Would you rather plan a surprise party for someone **OR** have someone plan a surprise party for you?

Would you rather listen to only Christmas music **OR** never be able to listen to it again?

Would you rather have an extremely cute Halloween costume **OR** an extremely scary Halloween costume?

WOULD YOU RATHER?

Would you rather find one Easter egg with twenty dollars inside **OR** a ton of Easter eggs overflowing with chocolate?

Would you rather watch fireworks **OR** set off fireworks on the Fourth of July?

Would you rather receive a secret Valentine **OR** send a secret Valentine?

MUSIC
&
MOVIES

Picking your favorite movie, actor, musician, or song is like choosing between endless flavors of ice cream – almost impossible! Whether you're jamming at home with your earbuds, or catching a movie, get ready to make some tricky decisions!

WOULD YOU RATHER?

Would you rather
be an extra **OR** the main
character in your favorite
movie?

Would you rather
listen to the same song on
repeat while you're getting
ready for school **OR** get ready
in silence for the next
three years?

Would you rather
watch only animated
movies **OR** action movies
forever?

WOULD YOU RATHER?

Would you rather know the lyrics to every song **OR** famous quotes from every movie?

Would you rather star in a romantic movie with your celebrity crush **OR** in a comedy with your best friend?

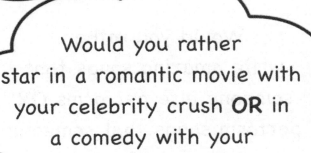

Would you rather play a superhero **OR** a villain in a movie?

WOULD YOU RATHER?

Would you rather live in the magical world of a fantasy movie **OR** the spooky world of a horror movie?

Would you rather write amazing songs that someone else performs **OR** perform songs that someone else wrote for you?

Would you rather create a new genre of music **OR** be able to play any song on the piano?

WOULD YOU RATHER?

Would you rather
give up music **OR** movies
for an entire year?

Would you rather
be born with perfect pitch
OR amazing acting abilities?

Would you rather
tour the world as a pop
star **OR** win an award
for best actress?

WOULD YOU RATHER?

Would you rather watch a movie that makes you laugh **OR** makes you cry?

Would you rather see your favorite actor perform live in a play **OR** see your favorite musician perform live at a concert?

Would you rather act in your favorite movie **OR** dance in your favorite musical?

CELEBRITIES, FAMOUS PEOPLE & CHARACTERS

Where to even begin? Movie stars, musicians, books—famous favorites are endless, and choosing isn't easy, but it's fun! From the latest pop stars to legendary figures from history, who's your top pick?

WOULD YOU RATHER?

Would you rather meet your favorite celebrity only to discover they are unkind **OR** see them from afar but never meet them?

Would you rather become a werewolf **OR** a vampire?

Would you rather meet your favorite actor **OR** your favorite singer?

WOULD YOU RATHER?

Would you rather be an Olympic athlete **OR** a really famous singer?

Would you rather be part of a girl band **OR** a K-pop group?

Would you rather go back in time and meet Amelia Earhart **OR** meet your favorite First Lady?

WOULD YOU RATHER?

Would you rather
be trained by astronaut
Christina Koch to go into space
OR become Vice President
of the US?

Would you rather
spend the day with a bratty
teen actress **OR** a funny
80-year-old actress?

Would you rather
attend a protest with Greta
Thunberg **OR** spend the day in
Washington working with
your senator?

FEARS
&
PHOBIAS

Umm... why is that snake giving you the eye? Brace yourself for a world of creepy, gross, spooky, and super icky choices in this section. You might want to skip this, but if you're brave enough, proceed at your own risk!

WOULD YOU RATHER?

Would you rather
stand on the edge of a tall
cliff **OR** crawl through
a small, dark space?

Would you rather
go to a haunted house filled
with scary clowns **OR**
life-sized dolls?

Would you rather
stick your feet in a bucket
of big fish **OR** stick your hand
in a bowl of worms?

WOULD YOU RATHER?

Would you rather
face your biggest fear **OR**
struggle with it forever?

Would you rather
give a speech in front
of your whole school
OR go skydiving?

Would you rather
climb a ladder three stories
high **OR** crawl half a mile
through a tunnel?

WOULD YOU RATHER?

Would you rather have a cockroach **OR** a rat in your kitchen?

Would you rather observe sharks from a cage underwater **OR** hold a big hairy spider?

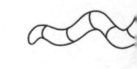

Would you rather come face-to-face with a king cobra **OR** a black bear while hiking?

WOULD YOU RATHER?

Would you rather spend one hour alone in an abandoned hospital during the day **OR** one hour alone in a cemetery at night?

Would you rather turn into a zombie **OR** a friendly ghost?

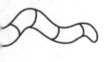

Would you rather have a tooth pulled out by the dentist **OR** get your blood drawn at the doctor's office?

WOULD YOU RATHER?

Would you rather spend an hour covered in spiders **OR** run a mile through spiderwebs?

Would you rather give a presentation in front of your whole school **OR** read your diary aloud to a bunch of strangers?

Would you rather get a facial where live snails crawl on your face **OR** a pedicure where little fish eat the dead skin on your feet?

WOULD YOU RATHER?

Would you rather dissect a frog in science class **OR** save it by taking it home and keeping it as a pet?

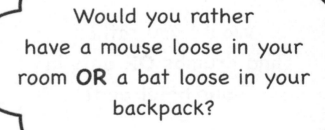

Would you rather have a mouse loose in your room **OR** a bat loose in your backpack?

Would you rather be on a plane lost in the atmosphere **OR** a submarine lost underwater?

WOULD YOU RATHER?

Would you rather sprinkle crickets in your smoothie **OR** June bugs on your pizza?

Would you rather find crumbs **OR** ants in your hotel bed?

Would you rather spend the night at your worst enemy's house **OR** in a haunted library?

WOULD YOU RATHER?

Would you rather walk around blindfolded all day **OR** with earplugs in all day?

Would you rather know there was a snake in your room but never see it **OR** have a toad living on top of your dresser?

Would you rather a creepy clown pop out of nowhere once a day **OR** a coyote cross your path once a day?

WOULD YOU RATHER?

Would you rather get food stuck in your hair **OR** find hair in your food at a restaurant?

Would you rather go cliff diving **OR** deep sea diving?

Would you rather live in a house used as the main set for a horror movie **OR** have a teacher who reminds you of a very scary villain from a movie?

FUNNY
&
SILLY

Every now and then, a little silliness can be a total blast, right? This "Would You Rather" book wouldn't be complete without a touch of the ridiculous. Prepare to have some fun!

WOULD YOU RATHER?

Would you rather only be able to taste lemon juice **OR** only be able to taste hot sauce?

Would you rather be able to know the future **OR** listen to people's thoughts?

Would you rather have a pet dragon **OR** a pet unicorn?

WOULD YOU RATHER?

Would you rather
have the ability to be
invisible **OR** see through
walls?

Would you rather
have a voice that sounds like
a little mouse **OR** a laugh that
sounds like a horn?

Would you rather
have a single eye **OR** a large
horn in the middle of
your head?

WOULD YOU RATHER?

Would you rather
fly on the back of
a friendly dragon **OR**
a sparkly unicorn?

Would you rather
spend the next week as
a two-year-old **OR**
a seventy-year-old?

Would you rather
sleep in a bed of moss **OR**
beach sand?

WOULD YOU RATHER?

Would you rather wear a green face mask all day at school for a year **OR** never be able to do another face mask again?

Would you rather swim in a pool filled with bath bombs **OR** ice cubes?

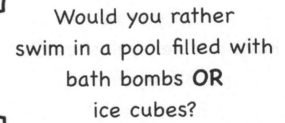

Would you rather post a face-swap selfie with your dad **OR** one with your dog?

WOULD YOU RATHER?

Would you rather bounce everywhere you go **OR** shuffle everywhere with your feet always on the ground?

Would you rather have purple eyelashes **OR** purple eyebrows for a week?

Would you rather have access to a magic lamp **OR** a magic carpet for a week?

WOULD YOU RATHER?

Would you rather get up every morning at 4:00 AM **OR** go to bed every night at 7:00 PM?

Would you rather be able to play the ukulele with your feet **OR** be able to walk on your hands for a long distance?

Would you rather live in a room full of butterflies **OR** hummingbirds?

WOULD YOU RATHER?

Would you rather have to walk backward everywhere you go **OR** do cartwheels to get around?

Would you rather have bubbles float out of your mouth every time you talk **OR** float out of your ears every time you listen?

Would you rather be able to breathe fire **OR** blow ice on command?

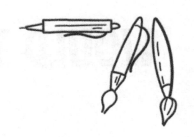

SCHOOL

Attention, principals and teachers – the students are taking charge! Ever dreamed of making a few school decisions? Now's your chance! It's all about fun, and there won't be any grades, promise!

WOULD YOU RATHER?

Would you rather have the ability to get good grades on a test without studying **OR** have someone do your homework for you?

Would you rather have all of your teachers like you **OR** all of your classmates like you?

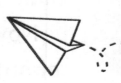

Would you rather get a bad grade after doing your best work **OR** get a good grade when you turn in someone else's work?

WOULD YOU RATHER?

Would you rather switch to writing with your opposite hand **OR** write upside down?

Would you rather have a cute uniform **OR** a casual dress code for school?

Would you rather absorb all knowledge of a book just by touching it **OR** understand all school subjects automatically?

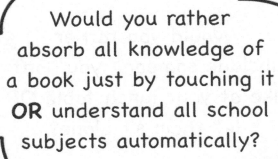

WOULD YOU RATHER?

Would you rather start **OR** end the day with your favorite class?

Would you rather have no homework **OR** no tests ever again?

Would you rather include someone you don't like at your lunch table **OR** let them sit alone?

$\sqrt{5^2}$

WOULD YOU RATHER?

Would you rather have your class outside in the snow **OR** inside, but you have to stand all day?

Would you rather get straight A's without studying **OR** be a star athlete without practicing?

Would you rather go to school through the entire year and graduate high school at 14 **OR** take the summers off and graduate high school at 18?

$\sqrt{5^2}$

WOULD YOU RATHER?

Would you rather scrub the school toilets **OR** wash every dish in the cafeteria after lunch?

Would you rather have a hall pass that you could use any time all year long **OR** leave school fifteen minutes early every day?

Would you rather never have to create a school project **OR** never have to take another math test?

WOULD YOU RATHER?

Would you rather trade places with your teacher **OR** with the principal?

Would you rather take a nap for an hour in the middle of the school day **OR** watch TV for an hour in the middle of the school day?

Would you rather be caught sneezing in your school yearbook photo **OR** have your hair sticking straight up?

WOULD YOU RATHER?

Would you rather make a new discovery in science class **OR** create a masterpiece in art class?

Would you rather be the captain of the chess club **OR** the head of the theater club?

$E=MC^2$

Would you rather burp the alphabet **OR** dance in front of the whole school?

ABOUT THE AUTHOR

Alexa Schlesinger is from Los Angeles and has fun playing volleyball, basketball, and dancing. Between school and activities, she loves planning holiday festivities and the next family birthday bash. She's known to bring a smile to her friends and family with her delicious baking and silly jokes, and will always kickstart the fun when the energy is low.

Alexa collaborated with some of her most creative friends to write "Would You Rather, For Girls, By Girls" when she was ten years old because she was obsessed with making up Would You Rather questions to try on friends and family.

Thanks for reading! Did you like the book?
I'd LOVE to hear! Reviews are super helpful for
independent authors like me, and I'd really appreciate it if
you left a review on Amazon - or even if you just scan the
code and give it a star rating, that would be great too!
Thanks for being a jokester friend!

FOR MORE WOULD YOU RATHER FUN

check out
"Would You Rather,
For Kids, By Kids" by silly duo
Alexa Schlesinger and
Jada Jacobelli!
Available on Amazon.

Made in United States
Orlando, FL
26 September 2024

51997582R00068